The Bed the Size of a Small Country

The Bed the Size of a Small Country

Poems by

Lois Marie Harrod

© 2025 Lois Marie Harrod. All rights reserved.
This material may not be reproduced in any form, published,
reprinted, recorded, performed, broadcast,
rewritten, or redistributed without
the explicit permission of Lois Marie Harrod.
All such actions are strictly prohibited by law.

Cover design by Shay Culligan
Cover art "The Bed the Size of a Small Country"
by Sarah Lacy
Author photo by Katherine C. Harrod

ISBN: 978-1-63980-779-6

Kelsay Books
502 South 1040 East, A-119
American Fork, Utah 84003
Kelsaybooks.com

For my husband of 57 years
Lee V. Harrod
1942–2022

For our children Jon and Kate

For our grandchildren Will, James, Sophie, and Sam

For the hundreds of students Lee taught in his 40 joyous years
as an English Professor at The College of New Jersey

For our dear friends and family members
who continue to enrich my life

Acknowledgments

Thank you to the following publications, in which versions of these poems previously appeared:

Adanna: "Happy Marriage"
After Happy Hour, a Journal of Literature and Art: "What I Understand Now"
California Quarterly: "Night Is Different Now"
The MacGuffin: "Identification"
The Main Street Rag: "How the Bed Fell Apart" as "How Things Fall Apart"
Origami Poems Project: "A Limited List of Ordinary Things," "After Your Ashes," "Forgiveness," "How can the heart," "The Dead Are Quiet," "This White Stone"
The Paterson Review: "What's Left"
Presence: a Journal of Catholic Poetry: "the light that persists even if"
Raleigh Review: "At This Point Love Boomerangs"
The Rat's Ass Review: "It now seems to me that I am the book I was talking about . . . ," "The brilliance that made all life possible becomes the cold stars"
Ravens Perch: "Because I could not believe in the resurrection," "Where You Can Find Me"
South Florida Poetry Journal: "Ode to My House That Has Come to Resemble a Funeral Parlor"
The Stillwater Review: "The Slant of Smile"
Terrain: "The Bed the Size of a Small Country"
US 1 Worksheets 69: "All it takes," "Smooth and White"
Wilderness House Poetry Review: "Sleeping with Love as He Grows Old," "Sometimes," "The dead can make any song come on the radio," "The Sky Unraveling Another Season"

Also by Lois Marie Harrod

Spat (Finishing Line Press, 2021)
Woman (2019 Blue Lyra Chapbook Contest, 2020)
Nightmares of the Minor Poet (Five Oaks, 2016)
And She Took the Heart (Casa de Cinco Hermanas Press, 2016)
Fragments from the Biography of Nemesis (Word Tech: Cherry Grove Collections, 2013)
How Marlene Mae Longs for Truth (Concrete Wolf, 2013)
The Only Is (*Poems & Plays* Tennessee Chapbook Contest, 2012)
Brief Term (Black Buzzard Press, 2011)
Cosmogony (2010 Hazel Lipa Chapbook, Iowa State, 2010)
Furniture (Grayson Press, 2008)
Firmament (Finishing Line Press, 2007)
Put Your Sorry Side Out (Concrete Wolf, 2005)
Spelling the World Backward (Palanquin Press, 2000)
This Is a Story You Already Know (Palanquin Press, 1999)
Part of the Deeper Sea (Palanquin Press, 1997)
Green Snake Riding (New Spirit Press, 1994)
Crazy Alice (Belle Mead Press, 1991)
Every Twinge a Verdict (Belle Mead Press, 1987)

Also by Lois-Marie Harrod

Contents

Bed Without a Comforter	15
The Bed the Size of a Small Country	17
How the Bed Fell Apart	18
Before he died	20
Sleeping with Love as He Grows Old	21
The Minor Poet Becomes Caretaker	22
Where We Were Now	23
Losing you	24
"the light that persists even if"	25
On Sleeping Alone	26
How to Say Goodbye in Any Language	27
When I weep now you are gone,	28
After Your Ashes	29
"Tu Es Partout"	30
"The dead can make any song come on the radio"	31
At This Point Love Boomerangs	33
Night Is Different Now	34
Ode to My House That Has Begun to Resemble a Funeral Parlor	36
What I Understand Now	41
Once I Argued with Another	43
Smooth and White	44
Now That I Know Nothing	46
Places Emptied of Words	47
Great Novel of Grief	48
How can the heart	49
Where You Can Find Me	50
The verb in the present tense is always alone	51
What's Left	52
"the brilliance that made all life possible becomes the cold stars"	53

"It now seems to me that I am the book I was talking about . . ."	55
A Limited List of Ordinary Things	56
Identification	57
Because I could not believe in the resurrection—	58
Of course,	59
The Dead Are Quiet	61
Forgiveness	62
All it takes—	63
Happy Marriage	64
Let there be no more plotting	66
The Slant of Smile	67

Bed Without a Comforter

I sleep, yes, sleep my gift,
but I slept too long, through too much,

I slept and did not know
you were going—and now

I want you to know me, sleeping
with these silly stuffed animals,

big bear, little bear,
river horse, new white kitten,

once my body, your body, our body
lumping in the bed,

bumped into being, then snoring,
you snored a lot—

I know you can't hear me—
why do I think otherwise?

Why did I think you
would snuffle up from sheets forever?

You rose so often those last years
I thought it was the resurrection—

but as foretold, the tomb is empty,
the stone gone cold.

I leave lights on. I go back
to sleep in your Marcel Proust t-shirt—

all that coming and going,
perhaps you trying to teach me—

coming and going,
coming and leaving.

The Bed the Size of a Small Country

*Wyndam Garden Philadelphia International Airport Hotel,
July 27, 2022*

What am I doing here at the edge
of this wide land, sheeting beyond me,
hills like overstuffed pillows
guarding the north border, or is it west?

I am having difficulty with directions
since you left, though once I was the navigator,
and you the driver who sometimes
didn't seem to know *north* from *drought,*

south from *sought,* but yes, we always found laughter
in the deserts—and I thought you were coming
with me, and now I am having trouble figuring out
just why I am or how I am going

or where to lay my head in these vacant hills.
Seven pillows, count, and not one yields.
Sitting here at the edge, I look at myself
in a mirror the size of a small lake,

a small woman huddled in a barren place
though someone said, *Don't look in the glass,
you'll get pregnant.* Like Abraham's Sarah,
I suppose, at ninety. Still ten years for that.

How the Bed Fell Apart

One day when he gets out of the car
he cannot straighten and you become

the one who lifts the suitcases
and hauls them up the stairs to the bed,

and sometimes he looks at you as if
he hasn't heard you, lately so often

that afterwards you will wonder
why you did not understand

how sick he was, maybe the last two, three years,
his unfailing good humor, concealing laugh.

Oh, you knew he didn't like doctors,
you knew he wanted to control his life

and sometimes yours—as those who live
together a long time occasionally

need the other . . . otherwise,
though you knew that some changes

mean a kind of disappearance,
his concentration on ideas,

that fixity—who would he have been without that?
So you didn't understand what was happening,

even when the nurse in the ER said,
kidney failure, liver failure—

somehow, you thought he would get well again.

Before he died

that spring of spasm and seizure,
pain prowled back and thigh,

flushed sleep from cover;
low-level lightning twitched,

jerked his spine,
his crooked spine, and contiguous,

the skin wanted pearls where
the sheet stung raw—

Noli me tangere.
Don't touch me, he said.

No respite
for weeks. Continuous.

Sleeping with Love as He Grows Old

He tosses but cannot turn,
something has happened to his spine,
to each little vertebra, to the nerves,
sciatic and femoral, something desperate,
isn't Love supposed to grow stronger, not weaker?

Love tries, but no chance to rest,
he's up a thousand times a night, his prostate
now larger than his heart and his heart,
that huge organ he promised forever,
is failing too, the San Andreas Fault—
Etna, Vesuvius, Love's lava growing cold.

Didn't he do what he ought, practice
what he preached?—oh he was so kind, watched his diet,
exercised like a madman cycling the globe.

Oh, Love, what have you done,
your body thin as a sheet?
Dickinson said you *can do all but raise the dead,*
and now you cannot raise a finger.

The Minor Poet Becomes Caretaker

Even mild-mannered Clark Kent
gets grumpy when the abscess
between his 4th and 5th vertebrae
bursts like the South Fork Dam
and breeches the little town
that inhabits his cheek.

Cheek? Oh, maybe *butt? buttock?*
booty? bum? keister? seat?
Let's call it *a glut*
of staphylococcus in the glutes.

Her *übermensch* is *under the weather*
and not impressed by her wit,
can't walk, can't fly,
can't fake his placid smile,
Supermuse is super sick—

And his excruciating infection has taken
longer to diagnose
than most poems to compose
though the minor poet,
whatever she manages to write,
wants his saga of suffering exposed
in dactylic hexameter
in the *New York Times Magazine.*

Face it, whispers her brave man,
some things should not be written
even if one 20th century poet did eulogize
her father's phlegm swirling in a glass
as a model of the solar system
writhing around the sun . . .

Where We Were Now

We were in a small boat
on a rough sea,
going to an island
where it seemed
someone was lonely,
and when the boat
skidded onto shore,
the gravel beach too
seemed floating
on a green fog
through the rain.
When we entered the house,
it became a dwelling
of many rooms,
chamber after chamber
of heavy chairs and beds
and dust-laden curtains,
and finally we saw them—
an old woman
hobbling towards us,
pushing her old man
curled in a wheelchair.
She seemed happy to see us,
offered hard cider and cheese,
but soon a voice said,
it seemed to be
the voice of the boat,
We must leave now
the weather is getting worse.

Losing you

as others have said, *easy*.
Difficult, saving you
and saving again,
those trips to the ER
you riding, shot gone,
or those sponge baths
with you hunched on the toilet,
hanging onto the bathtub rail,
your broad back, how carefully
I washed the sweet places
I once had known in sweeter ways—
oh, I was new to this,
clumsy, you would
call me when you were ready,
after you somehow managed
to stand and shave.

After you died, I came
to the hospital bed and ran
my wrist over your beard
until it was raw.

"the light that persists even if"

Kevin Young, "Ledge"

It was strange,
another widow told me,
*TJ died and the world
continued, the sun
slipped up and slid down
and did not stop
for me.*

I stood at the edge
of sky, days diminishing
one by one
as if they could not
notice I was there.

I remembered
my preacher father
inviting
every man
with a thumb in the air
into the front seat
of his car,
proselytizing
while my sister
and I sat hushed
in the back.

On Sleeping Alone

Mostly someone in bed beside me,
my sister Mary all our childhood,
two in the bed, arguing whose side,
ready to sever the foot that strayed.

And then with you for 57 years
in that little oak four-poster—
the one we bought after graduate school
at Moses Used Furniture
on Hermitage Avenue.
We never asked
who slept there
before we dreamed.

Nor in those last years together
did I think that I would miss
your groaning
out of bed 5 or 6 times a night,
or my lying awake
waiting for you to start again
to breathe.

I stuff your side with pillows
and the teddy bear I bought
when you became so sick.

How to Say Goodbye in Any Language

I wrote my farewells to my father
before he died, well, what can I say?

All those weekends driving
to Walnut Creek, Ohio, and then writing

a poem each return, a whole book,
because it was a long dying, oh, those diseases

that don't slam the door, that leave the cold
air seeping in—Alzheimer's, Parkinson's,

dementia, and cancer too with its remitted
arrivederci, I'll be back but you, another story,

no time to say goodbye, not a goodbye
you could hear.

When I weep now you are gone,

I sometimes remember
my father's book

where sorrow was a sin
and joy . . . silliness.

We could be jubilant,
but let's tamp down

the glee.
Something Grinchy

about salvation—
God's grace, yes,

but don't brag.
Dad didn't like it either

when we dervished
until we were dizzy,

convulsed in giggles
on the rug.

As for fountains of tears,
he had no more compassion

than Picasso
for weeping women.

You weren't always sure either,
my dear, what to do

when I wept.

After Your Ashes

bats with umbrella wings flit by
and then the shush of rain

sheathing the meadow grass.
Don't cry, you say again

so I hang the spider string
of wet beads on the yarrow

where flea beetles flit
with gnats.

Once again I bought
more pears than I can eat

and sit in the kitchen
with the fruit flies—

the kitchen
where you loved to be

making your bread and cheese
and soupy things,

singing *Hard-hearted Hannah*
while I stood slack and smiling

the vamp of Savannah
slumming with the coffee rings.

"Tu Es Partout"

Suddenly you are in the house again
sitting in your chair, reading—

your battered copy of *Finnegans Wake*—
your reappearance his redundancy.

Isn't that how we learn to grieve, but
did you think I haven't been here all along?

Look up and you might see me
wondering once again

what you loved more than me.
I have always loved you

you said the second time
to the emergency ward.

The third, bringing you
the third time, I said,

See I have saved your life,
Finnegan, you who did not love doctors.

How you loved Edith Piaf
though sometimes I could barely bear

the agony of her voice—
now I listen to hear you.

"The dead can make any song come on the radio"[1]

Hilda was an old friend, in her fifties when we met her
on the sidewalk of Riverside Avenue, and she told us
how to get to Sears where we needed to buy a bed
if we didn't want to sleep on the floor at 518,
our first and first-floor apartment with a toilet on a dais.

And though Hilda seemed to like me at first,
she found more and more to disapprove of as the years
went by, as she made herself our local grandma—
I was drab, she said, I didn't wear bright clothes, I didn't
eat enough because I worried about my figure,
I went about cooking the dinner to which we had invited her
instead of sitting in the living room conversing
as her etiquette required even though
I was putting the last turnips in her vegetarian glop.
She seemed to expect me to wave
a magic wand and zap her overcooked eggs,
let the rice burn as the salad tossed itself.

So death became all about food—I know, a big leap—
but she was *fat* because this was the 70s, before
the demise of *stout, portly, obese, big,*
and Hilda was always on one diet or other,
every summer giving up her fresh peaches
with their cruel carbs, and bananas, those brutal bananas—
as for me, I ate peaches while she decided I was anorexic,

but, that was another story
Hilda did not want to hear, and so I did not tell her I had
counted calories every day since I was in sixth grade
because who wants to hear about a father who sings

---

[1] "What the Dead Can Do," Oliver Baez Bendorf, "They [the dead] can make any song come on the radio."

*I don't want her, you can have her, she's too fat
for me* all the way to Baltimore with that 40s song blaring
on the radio in that 1939 Ford where I sat squashed
in the back seat between my two skinny sisters,

because who wants to hear about Bobby Jones,
that boney blue-eyed rat, who said *You 'ain't nothing but a fatso*
that day when I told my teacher Mrs. McKee
that she needed to read from books about famous women
as well as that big one of hers about famous men. *All the boys
hate you,* said Bobby as we waited in line
for round little Mr. Basil to open the music room door.

So I do believe the dead or the dying
can do some things like continue to shout
the nasty things they said, but when Hilda told me
she now had proof of everlasting life,
I told her that I refused to believe.

Seems that before her friend Connie died of cancer
Hilda had asked her for a sign. *Send me a sign,* she said,
sitting beside Connie in Helene Fuld Hospital,
Send me a sign that there is life after death,
and sure enough three days later that radio which hadn't worked
for years, like most of the electric objects
stacked neck-high in that house of Hilda's, mysteriously
popped on when a semi rumbled by on Route 29
and that was ample proof, she said,
Connie was alive, there was an eternity.

She turned it on, Hilda said.
and it was playing *Big Bottom*
which must have been proof of something.

At This Point Love Boomerangs

I am just trotting down the street
minding my busyness—

red stiletto to the shin—
no stopping to say *oh, so surly.*

    *

Or I'm wildebeesting
from the Serengeti to Masai Mara

and a crocodile jaws my hock
and I begin limping towards the riverbank

when a lion rushes the grass
to gnaw my heart

    *

Or I pick up James Joyce's *Ulysses*
filled with your cramped scribbles—

no Rosetta Stone to translate
the glyphs.

    *

And this old shopping list—
did you scrawl *Gouda* or *Gone?*

Night Is Different Now

December 7, 2023

I let little lights glimmer all over the house
the way God—if I suppose a god—
forgets to turn off his stars—

an extravagant way of keeping my way
in way of the dark.

The fluorescent light, you remember,
above the kitchen sink, I now call Sirius
which in 1844 the German astronomer
Friedrich Bessel noticed had a wobble,

(you would like such specificity),

and a little later in 1862
Alvan Clark discovered why:

the old Dog Star was not one star but two—

something I guess we knew
about marriage
without a telescope.

It's 51 years since we moved into this
little house of ours
and that shaky fluorescent tube
is still sifting over the sink—

I don't think we ever replaced it—

And now I let it shillyshally
through night and day,
as if you were still
dillydallying here with me.

Ode to My House That Has Begun to Resemble a Funeral Parlor

The melancholy transformation began this spring—
or when I decided though not yet spring, it should be spring—

I was seeing rank upon rank of plants at the grocery store, plants impatient for spring—
impatient impatiens, those shady lovers, and I had seen enough shades recently

to populate perdition, too many stamens like ghosts, *What man stays? No man,*
Nemo, Stay, Man, Stay. I bought some for my window.

To counter the Law of Contraries, I bought sun-lovers too, the Law of Agreement,
pink petunias and Shasta daisies with faces a little too happy

not to contain sorrow, white begonias and yes, desiccated daffodils
which will return to life next spring after a winter rot in their pots.

So I bought flowers, lots of flowers, the ones that don't need too much attention,
which is the way I've always chosen flora, sometimes fauna, yes even friends,

knowing the needy are Venus flytraps, waiting to suck the milli-ounce of insect blood,
knowing too, some demanding flowers flourish without taking more of me

than an ice cube thrown in their direction once a week.
Look at this delicate orchid on my windowsill: it's bloomed

four times in the last three years and this time, 22 blossoms.
The Law of Contraries, *odi et amo,* oh my Catullus, I loved you
    most of the time . . .

as I loved that orchid which first bloomed lilac, a pale orchid
    ballerina,
then turned boy, blossoms with pale boy faces

and purple freckles, trans-flowers, the way we are all shift male to
    female,
woman to man, strong to needy, reliant to self-reliant,

but let's leave those distinctions for floral philosophers, those fools
who may or may not tell us this too is a corollary of the Funeral
    Home Effect.

And then because I was feeling rather brave and *funereal,* or was it
    grave
and *fun, really funny,* what are you reeling now wherever you are
    or not?—

except I know you aren't here because your ashes remain in the
    guest bedroom.
I don't know what to do with them.

Before you died, we joked about my hiking solo five miles into the
    Wyoming Big Horns
and dusting the lupins and Indian paint brush with what is left of
    you.

I think that was the plan, because you always said you'd die first,
    and then you did,
as if you had to be faithful to your word,

and now I am 80, and a bit hesitant to set out for the high hills
alone.

So because you are no longer here to *hear* my incessant babble,
notice I don't say *listen to,* you didn't always, I decided to buy cut
    flowers too,

carnations, that stalwart funeral flower, they last weeks—a bit like
    grief.
And yes, I bought yellow carnations, too late for your white sports
    coat

and pink incarnation, which hasn't happened either . . . no, these
    are pale yellow
and I won't call them *sickly yellow* because they have already
    lasted for three and a half weeks.

A few are getting a bit brown around the frills—
not unlike the big bruise on my knee where I tripped up the stairs.

Oh, I shouldn't have been wearing those clunky unisex Crocs,
unisex—another way of being dead, nothing sexy about Crocs,

but my knee is the shade of shades, no sex in heaven, OMG,
a bruise the size of a peony—green and yellow and purple and
 blue.

I know, I know, you told me once, more than once, I shouldn't
 wear those shoes,
though I was listening without hearing and once again proved you
 right or wrong.

Well, I have survived the fall and am surviving in this house of
 flowers—so many,
too many, and just as I was ready to plant them deep in the earth,
 aching knee and all,

I got COVID. I stayed in bed, no flower bed for me this week, no
 bed of roses,
but people kept dropping bouquets on the porch for me to take in
 and tend.

Flowers now from one end of the house to the other, kitchen, living
 room, bedroom—
wine-red calla lilies, blue chrysanthemum daisies, ghostly
 begonias, Eurydice's coleus.

Last night my doorbell rang, the one that plays *Hymn to Joy,*
the one I installed *all by myself* because I am learning to do a lot
 you used to do,

and at my door there he is, a godling, maybe 20, maybe 23 with
 dark hair
and obsidian eyes. And he is holding out a bouquet of red roses and
 red chrysanthemums,

deep red with a spray of baby breath, another aspect, I suppose, of
   that wall of contraries
I keep falling from, into, and I say, *Oh my God, how beautiful.*

And he says, as if he were Hermes, as if he were Eros, as if he
   were Hades himself,
yes—as if he were you, *Happy Mother's Day, Love.*

Love, that fleeted-footed messenger with the beat-up van, the one
   that escorts us to the underworld, *Love,* he called me *Love,* and I
   think once again, *The wages of dying . . .*

The wages of dying is love.[2]

---

[2] Galway Kinnell, "Little Sleep-Head Spouting Hair in the Moonlight."

What I Understand Now

Those who keep
the room exactly as it was,
unmade bed, poster slack.

The ones who lie
beside the body
as it cools.

The ones who kiss
the crooked mouth.

    *

And, yes, later
the ones who pack up
the never-worn shirts
and the eight pairs of shoes
down in the heel.

Reeboks, the only ones
that ever fit
those Neanderthal feet of yours—

the sort Michelangelo
gave his prophet Daniel.

    *

At Rehab, Erica
told you to buy new sneakers—
imagining, I guess
your lumpy feet
suddenly sleek and fluorescent.

Next session
I dug your newest
black look-alikes
out of their closet box
and shoved them on.

    *

You preferred your books
to clothes—

though you liked it
when I bought something new,
always telling me
how lovely I looked.

Who will I ask now
when I walk into the living
room, "Am I okay?"

Once I Argued with Another

But you must hope, he said
as if hope were a pill
that could slide down the throat.

You must have faith, he said
as if faith were a triple-bypass
that would repair the heart.

And you must love, he said,
the only panacea I thought
possible, a dose of charity

which as Emily Dickinson knew
despite her *thing with feathers*
can *do all but raise the dead*

and, she says, could do that
if flesh were not so weak.
I am tired, I said,

perhaps tomorrow I can love
but today to stop weeping,
I must sleep.

Smooth and White

the stone you gave me,
wrapped my fingers round

as if you were cradling
your heart

in my hand.
Keep it safe, you said.

It was that brief
afternoon

you lay grieving
beside me.

I must go
you said, lingering

as the sick
sometimes do,

light you seemed
and leaving.

I wanted
you as stone

heavy on me,
hard and smooth—

I slip
this little pebble

under my tongue
to still myself.

Now That I Know Nothing

What do I say
when the old scats
I use as crutches
disappear?

After I learn
I am not a lilt
with a fragile sting?

After the gull slashes
my belly croon
and finds
a black marble,
a plastic wheel,
three sharps?

All those baleful rounds
I have not spit out—
and yet here I am alive
and singing.

Maybe just
a chemical thing,
a prickly burr
dissolving
in the craw.

If you want access
to my troll,
you must subscribe
to my grief.

Places Emptied of Words

Bridges emptied of trucks—
the spans my friend has trouble crossing—

Here, I say, I will drive
and you huddle in the back seat

with a mask over your eyes,
neither of us will say anything

until it is over.

*

Or porches voided of rocking chairs—
first grandfather's, then mother's

and now yours—
I do not know how to say good-bye

to anyone, I am not that man
who knew he was dying

and called his friends
one by one

until it was finished.

Great Novel of Grief

You thought you could skim through it,
your *Moby Dick of Sorrow,*

20,000 Leagues under the Brackish Sea,
didn't you read every word of *War and Peace?*

But here you are, halfway *usque ad finem*—
Old Woman and the Salty Sea.

The small print is pulling you under
with its seal and stamp,

punch and counter punch,
cheat and sleep.

Who flutter-kicks the leaden octopi—
you, who were always such a sucker for happy stories,

who believed you could float
into the belly of any old right whale

and emerge in Nineveh
where everyone you loved

would be waving gourd leaves above you
in the penultimate paragraph?

How odd the antonym of *salt*
is *sweet.*

How can the heart

on which everything depends
suddenly begin beating

like John Bonham battering
Moby Dick?

And why does it happen
in the middle of sudden grief—

this crazy stick pick licking
life, life, life

sudden whip-flip
in the middle of sadness?

Where You Can Find Me

Watching Love trite off into the sunset,
that dusty gaucho

making his exit, stock move in a stock movie:
Here comes the dusk, here come the credits.

Love you forever,
he said and left.

I stay to the end—
read the rolling print,

*the Second Assistant
to the On-Set Director—*

oh let the credits ride.
I believed

he would love me forever—
wasn't Love the lead?

Get along, little dogie,
I'm the last in the theatre.

*Lay still, little dogie,
stop roamin' around.*

No one left to come
to my mother's funeral either.

*It's your misfortune
And none of my own.*

The verb in the present tense is always alone

I live . . . I die . . . solitary as a star so far
beyond the telescope I can't find my beginning
except as I am continuing, the *I am living* . . .
the *I am dying* . . . but solitary in the past too . . .
you lived, you died . . . but sometimes in the tense
past and perfect, we ceased to be solitary:
I have not always been alone,
you were here sitting in your chair,
though when you were, I was often alone, each of us alone
you alone in your book wending your way
through its wilderness of words, though sometimes
suddenly, looking up, as if you could suddenly see me,
alone in my words, you'd tell me something
you were reading. *Sir Tristram, violer d'amores, fr'over*
the short sea, had passencore rearrived from
North Armorica on this side the scraggy isthmus[3]
and for a while I would listen and be less alone.

---

[3] James Joyce, *Finnegans Wake*

What's Left

Somedays I think those cargo pants of yours
must now be walking around Trenton or Jersey City

on another short little bald man, a bit overweight
like you, maybe with that wide leather belt of yours

holding up those heavy pockets filled with dog bones
on the left side and starlight mints on the right,

just in case we meet a friendly dog on our walks—
and we always did,

just in case you got what you called a "dizzy spell,"
one of those times you couldn't speak or walk for ten or fifteen
    minutes—

yes, scary and undiagnosed though we often tried,
though in that frantic third-to-last ER visit, a neurologist

got out his cell phone and said perhaps
it was some sort of very rare episodic ataxia.

Yes, those cargo pants must be out walking a rescue pit bull,
some of them are nice like Lucy, our son's Staffordshire mix,

who died the same weekend you did,
the same Father's Day weekend

our grandson Will tumbled 78 feet in a blizzard
off a mountain precipice in Southern Oregon

and somehow lived.

"the brilliance that made all life possible becomes the cold stars"

—Louise Glück, *October*

They say you are still here—
you know the *they* I mean,
the *they* who want to raise you
from the dead, so, I guess, you can
raise your eyebrows
and roll your blue eyes
at their belief.

They say you reached down
and saved our grandson,
you know the *they* I mean,
the *they* you always gave that sweet
enigmatic smile—
that's as far as that cold *Thou*
could take you to scoop them
from the cold unknown.

His fall—two days after you died.

And here I am,
your darling, your disbeliever,
talking as if you are here,
chattering in my blizzard of stars.

There was no resurrection,
no one rises from the dead,
but it is strange,
that alone, mountain-climbing
the weekend you died,
our grandson lost his way
in a sudden snow squall,
slipped off the mountain path,
fell 78 feet without losing
his tarp or his phone,
lay there all night, he told me afterwards,
thinking of those he loved—

as I keep thinking of you
my not-here *thou,*
my cold cold star.

"It now seems to me that I am the book I was talking about . . ."

Marcel Proust

You those last moments
wrapped in that silly hospital gown
with porpoises flipping this way and that,
tiny little porpoises
jumping all over your body,
the pummeling
our children Jon and Kate
gave you
when they crawled
into bed with us,
and then our grandchildren,
Sophie and Sam
flap-flopping all night
between us,
the fish in our line,
and Will and James sneaking
up the stairs
to crawl on top of you,
pretend you were their steed
to everywhere—
and you were—
as we each
carry each other
from the beginning
to the end,
that mystery . . .

A Limited List of Ordinary Things

the cargo pants with mended pockets
the three pairs of Reeboks with heels worn like a well-used eraser
the flannel-lined jacket with dog bones in the pocket
the aqua baseball hat from Barcelona
the grandfather coffee cup with Sam and Sophie in your arms
the wallet with your social security card
the passport that does not expire until 2031
the chair with the James Joyce's *Ulysses* margins
       crammed with your illegible scribbles
the five pounds of King Arthur whole wheat flour
the pound of yeast I bought for you from the local non-profit diner
       during the pandemic
the leather bedroom slippers that you thought too new to wear—

Identification

There's this little *chit*
I have been hearing
since you died—

I thought one of those flitty
brown feathers
difficult to sort from brown others

but today the *chit*
is as close as Cheryl's Rose of Sharon,
chit and hop to the next branch,

chit and hop to the ground,
chit and cock your head
at the hostas de-flowered by deer

and I can see now
it's the red cardinal with his black beak
like an exclamation point, *chit,*

and now that crazy crow
who sounds like he had a tracheotomy,
he's here too, cawing

and now the Carolina wren is singing
from farther away, *Where are you?*
Where are you?

and again his three-note,
I need you, I need you,
that I used to imitate

when we walked together.

Because I could not believe in the resurrection—

Oh, the past, you used to say,
forget it

but I did not,
my art, re-fleshing words

like some sort of Jesus
doing pop-up resurrections:

*Rise, take up thy bed
and stalk.*

And the odor of re-vivification—
Lazarus slouching from the tomb

smelling
like a corpse flower.

Some said I bathed my darlings
to scrub the rot away—

others, to make the pain
live forever.

Of course,

there was a man
with a fortune in words

ambassador
in every language

French, Russian,
English,

Swahili
Urdu, Romanian,

and he told me
in *strange iterations*

*love he would
ever for me*

and then he walked away——
the man

who appeared and disappeared
all my life—

off to India, off to Spain,
off to Singapore to play

Professor Henry Higgins
in *My Fair Lady,*

and yet I don't think
leaving is necessarily

the nature of erudite men.
You stayed, didn't you,

until your
faithful heart

stopped you in your endless
treks and tracts?

The Dead Are Quiet

They don't answer
when you ask

if they want a drink
or had a good *lay*.

They don't leave love notes
in the charnel house

reminding you
to warm the sheets

or turn off the light
or lock the coffin,

but you wake
in the middle of the night

hearing them
whisper

in an extinct language,
maybe Mycenean Greek.

Forgiveness

You broke the dessert bowls
we bought in Wellfleet
and could not replace
because the pottery disappeared—

and I broke the coffee cup
you bought for me in Provincetown
but you found another online
almost its replica—
so much easy giving, giving up, forgiving.

One person told me
I should forgive you too for dying.

All it takes—

for Lee, 1942–2022

slight slit, hairline crack
in the handmade cup,
the one I used for morning coffee,
that ceramic cup you bought me
young in Provincetown, the one you replaced
when it cracked years later,
sweet man who was mine,
57 years, the one who liked
to tell me things, the one
who liked to tell me how to do things
when my way was not
your way, that too, the one who said

Now don't put this new cup in the microwave,
though permission had been granted
by the potter, *microwave safe—*
the same no-fault insurance I granted you,
flaw by flaw, into most of my heart,
who among us is without sin?

And didn't I say, in defiance, *I will use this
cup, I won't leave it on the shelf
with those brandy snifters of yours,
the ones you do not want me to use
because I might break them,*
and yet how could you not know the clumsiness

that was me, wasn't I always
the flawed vessel, crack by crack, rift by rift,
a cup that could not hold all you wanted to pour?
*Oh, love, the cup is cracked again,
coffee seeping onto the kitchen floor.*

Happy Marriage

Of course, we were always imagining how it would end
with that flight to India when we were 102 or 108—

sudden loss of oxygen and drop to sea—
passing out before the death plunge

and years later when the seas would rise again
into dry lands, divers would find us

in Seats 21 A and B, still curled together, clutching hands.
And though you often said

in your dying months, we had lived through the best
of times, and true—our world was mostly kind,

though we did not ask as much as many,
kept our cars until there was no fixing,

and that clothes dryer spun 47 years without the now-necessary
   array
of dials and degrees in this little tract-house, mid-entry shack

as imperfect as us, walls once infested with yellow jackets,
and a driveway growing uneven as we bumbled across.

And, yes, sometimes I think about those spoons you used
to get your gobs of peanut butter and the knives and forks

you left on the counter and wished you would just once take them
to the dishwasher, which we replaced twice, but of course

you were thinking of something else, and I should have known
so much more than I did after our 57 years, should have

realized you were telling me that you thought you were dying
all those months when you were saying, *we've had a good run—*

those months long before the problem
was detected. *The future will be better tomorrow—*

who believes that? Even our neighbors who after all these
years now acknowledge the climate

is changing. "I never talk politics," they still say,
but the whole dying earth is political—as your death

was political—overworked doctors, quick assumptions,
stroke, heart attack, spine damage, episodic ataxia, finally

the cause, an undetected massive staph infection,
oh I am continuing, but you have no idea

how I miss your little lapses, your not noticing
I was the one who scrubbed the sink, the counter,

washed the clothes, folded your baggy briefs.

Let there be no more plotting

Let the sun rise and fall
like a continent

Let the blueberry
bog and barren

Let the monk seal fall asleep
in his habit of sand

Let the snow fall
until the clouds empty

Let the agave teeth
on its syrup, heal our wounds

Let the wind wring
the bristlecone like a rag

Oh, the ice patterns on the Dneiper—
something a Braque could copy

Let the hooded merganser
display above the water

like a priest
blessing the Black Sea

Let the black birds of anguish
bless all who flee

The Slant of Smile

at the bedroom door,
the crinkled smug of sleep—
oh my deep, made of flowers,

how do we last to the last
when the present prods past?

Yesterday a parchment of poses
on which to slip my love—
today, the smirk of crows.

It will be like all things we know[4]
Beaks will break; backs repose.

No croaking when we crowd
the boneyard gate
where every sheet's a shroud.

---

[4] from Arna Bontemps's "Length of Moon"

About the Author

Lois Marie Harrod is the author of eighteen other poetry collections. She received five fellowship-residencies from the Virginia Center for Creative Arts and three fellowships from the New Jersey Council on the Arts. Hundreds of her poems and several short stories have been published in literary journals and online ezines from *American Poetry Review* to *Zone 3*.

A Dodge poet, she has read four times at Geraldine R. Dodge Poetry Festivals. In the last 20 years, Harrod, a life-long educator, has taught creative writing at The College of New Jersey, literature courses at the Evergreen Forum of the Center for Modern Aging Princeton, as well as poetry-writing workshops for Murphy Writing and classroom residencies.

Find links to her online work at:
loismarieharrod.org

www.ingramcontent.com/pod-product-compliance
Lightning Source LLC
Chambersburg PA
CBHW071227200426
R18167400001B/R181674PG43193CBX00001B/1